Of Mongrelitude

Of Mongrelitude

JULIAN TALAMANTEZ BROLASKI

WAVE BOOKS SEATTLE AND NEW YORK

PUBLISHED BY WAVE BOOKS

WWW.WAVEPOETRY.COM

COPYRIGHT © 2017 BY JULIAN TALAMANTEZ BROLASKI

ALL RIGHTS RESERVED

WAVE BOOKS TITLES ARE DISTRIBUTED TO THE TRADE BY

CONSORTIUM BOOK SALES AND DISTRIBUTION

PHONE: 800-283-3572 / SAN 631-760X

LIBRARY OF CONGRESS CATALOGING-IN-PUBLICATION DATA

NAMES: BROLASKI, JULIAN T., AUTHOR.

TITLE: OF MONGRELITUDE / JULIAN TALAMANTEZ BROLASKI.

DESCRIPTION: FIRST EDITION. | SEATTLE : WAVE BOOKS, [2017]

IDENTIFIERS: LCCN 2016033162 | ISBN 9781940696454 (LIMITED

EDITION HARDCOVER) | ISBN 9781940696447 (SOFTCOVER)

CLASSIFICATION: LCC PS3602.R6425 A6 2017 | DDC 811/.6—DC23

LC RECORD AVAILABLE AT HTTPS://LCCN.LOC.GOV/2016033162

PRINTED IN THE UNITED STATES OF AMERICA

9 8 7 6 5 4 3 2 1

FIRST EDITION

WAVE BOOKS 062

This book is for my friends

I love you with everything in me

Of Mongrelitude

[WAR MESSAGE!]
we dont want yr tools

look gentlepeople
the only source of likelihood
is a fist in a gentle orifice
if I'da been a ranch
they'da calld me bar none
a fecund desert
full of heartless so-and-sos
the tub of butter thereafter was rancid
we put xir and xir mouth ta rest
along with the chickens in our maw
hey blood, hey sucka
as like to one as to th'other
do you love your sibling
as they do   as they do

against breeding

FOR CACONRAD

garbage-gut humans should not continue ourselves

it can only come a frightful cropper

hairbulbs what I mistook to be   a form in nature

albatross w/ plastics crowding thir gut

what julie patton is callin *superfraja-lilly-of-the-valley*

veronica heterophilia   *snapdraggon nature preserve*

pulp them   shropshire constabulary

quing of haven   sailing for caracas   sissy jesus-hag

point to the exact place where the fly shd go   in the ballo underpants

just where the shapes   come to a point triangularly

15 thousand fish dead at the mouth of tha mississipp

planes go sipsip   saying to the poor people

walk fa-ast!   walk like yr on hot co-als!

matisse had to get up real close   to see that was a burd

turned that viol de gamba right fwds   & added a noose

even more clîché than   peaches inna bowl

curvy long pear stem and   butterdish suspended

in air   perhaps the stem is penetrating a clear butter dish

conrad suggested   & I knew I was being drawn

into a funhouse of mirrors but I cdnt stop

odilon   redon   roger & angelica

why I am against breeding

rather like a doubting dog

I performed my own rejection of the species,
Rather like a doubting dog
perhaps I was so earnest in my approach
it appeared too regular,
not like an approach at all
betimes I discovered an odd pair of bruises,
a burnmark and a lesser one
as if the portals for psychic vampires
wound in twos, side by side
perhaps my suffering—but away
w/ phrases that begin perhaps
my suffering! still—it—

in the cut

FOR CEDAR SIGO

his being punished / for talking Indian.
—CEDAR SIGO, 'Prince Valiant'

person of clear salt water
warm clear deer

the mosquitoes I am
delicious to them
because of my fairy
or my indian blood

he is immune
to poison ivy
because indians dont
call it poison

utter unfaith in humanity
leaves dont turn right
the leaves so that
they dont know how to turn right

when the guy at the bodega
complained about white ppl & gentrifications
you said me and my friend are native
I'm Suquamish, look it up

I vaporize the weed
we had for breakfast when
I come home from the poetry reading
thinking how low & how lively
we know of the cut

droppd my parasol in a ditch
pretend it didnt happen

on loneliness

when the rains finally came, they were relentless
the ground, unaccustomed to moisture
after years of drought, was forced to reject
the thing it craved the most
and floods peopled our every vein and the
cracked riverbed wept——its tears ran down——w/out feeling——
like whiskey off a duck's back
truly complementary colors make a neutral
if I was made to remark
the polar vortex is strong in you
perhaps it wasn't so much
the oscillation in us
of some kind of arctic impulse
or oceanic feeling
toward what I perceive to be our relation
but rather, as always, it was my own
projection or transference or ocular
hallucination——which one can see is a pleasurable labor——
——silk pricked out with gold——
orange and blue is the exception——tho
they are complements, together they made a green, not muddy n/t
I was awake enough to be grossed out by your joke

but in a nice way, like a dog delights to tramp about in mud
Deborah says that Love entails the danger of destruction
whose heat humps thru the bedsheets
like a black hole bends the universe
or a mass is wracked along a frame
when the skunk sneaks in bed with the dog, ugh s(w)oon it has to hold
its nose, and eventually the violence, it flings the skunk
in disgust to the curb
funny, except the distress is authentic
say righteousness is an impulse toward being comely
just ask the one smurfette
how is she supposed to fend off all those smurves
or wtf cd a feminism even mean in that context
where everyone is blue
except gargamel and azrael, thinly veiled evil jew and cat antagonists
vocal fry making sad heron noises
headed to zorgonia off the x line in queens
profound experience of missing out
gillyham, arden, cokaygne, up to my neck in shit for seven years
the ramshackle succulents were about to bloom
we are engemmed in Victorian England
by virtue of Sherlock's mind palace
the horses
chewing thru the narration
were authentic, scooby-doo was authentic, Lozen was authentic, its hearts
were haunted as in
a pavilion where you pay with meat
our gazes cross, unmet
D. says that loneliness is a disbelief
in the possibility of Love
I hid it so well
I hid it from myself

no ordinary sorrow
but—say righteousness is impassable along a pollen path
a belief in being comely
a kodachrome you would take from me
along w/ the ill-fitting hats
and my belief in myself
as some kind of speculative cartography—
       composed of trees
              intermittent mountains
                      dope caballiers
—except the distress is authentic

—

Cokaygne: 'The Land of Cokaygne,' 14th-century utopic nonsense poem (http://www.thegolden
    dream.com/landofcokaygne.htm)
Lozen: Chihenne Chiricahua Apache two-spirit warrior, contemporary of Geronimo
pollen: for Apaches, (yellow cattail) pollen is sacred and used in prayer and ceremony
The distress is authentic: line of dialogue about a wooden barrel on a beach, from the film *Fort Tilden*
The effect [of isolation] can be almost completely irreversible lack of development of whole systems, such as those necessary
    for the use of vision in accomplishing tasks put to the animal (Frieda Fromm-Reichmann, 'Loneliness').
The more severe developments of loneliness appear in the unconstructive, desolate phases of isolation and real loneliness
    which are beyond the state of feeling sorry for oneself—the states of mind in which the fact that there were people in
    one's past life is more or less forgotten, and the possibility that there may be interpersonal relationships
    in one's future life is out of the realm of expectation or imagination ('Loneliness,' emphasis
    mine).

I did it for something to do

I did it for something to do
flimsy as fishbones
I did it for something to do
wrackd eche sentiment brevily

and verily
I do it for you are like the rook
er—or like a brook
whos aspect suddenly manifest as stream
to which I take my cigarettes & pie & all the bones of all the chicken
and toss them in
because you dont care for me

dont talk to me abt the amazon
I did it for something to hook
false and fine love meet their snakelike passage in the swamp
& the monobreasted creatures
cdnt tell the difference between
the furies whos eyes were wet w/ tears
and the ottoperson
dribbling beer out its one good nostril

fire place

whos hooves henceforth clasped
western bluebird
denied a certain cerulean
legitimacy
used to it
as worms
coming up thru moss
nibble the peyote
like corn on the cob
who nickname the fire
backside-be-cold-no-more

most honeyed

*something was getting ready to relax into a $4.00 ice cream sandwich when someone
placed a personal pronoun directly on p., that whatever had abandoned years ago.*
—KARI EDWARDS, a day in the life of p.

that most ~~that~~ honeyed ~~form chi~~
~~that~~ took xemself
up against knocks   n set ^(to be met) ~~to meet~~ / against (incontro)
with-for——that so being forse achen
upon my word, srsly
ich have litel worth (^[or] had not the thot)
to thereby go ariding & YET have (hath) ridden forsooth my hyde
þat one is said to have been and must to remain one way
it ~~has~~ hath been forwilled my brayne aches like lyke a goat
        litel company   no forsooth it ~~has~~ hath forgone,
that is it is forwent, having been gone, passed over
to be ~~erst~~ all-the-while forsaken, though the lover ~~was~~ is
    perhaps there ys s/t (suthing) in the populace
that speaks for, may be here-as-here ^y wis. ~~why~~ ^what sayestou
that itys locked   —& now n—now being asked to re-whoa why ought ^(n't)
(that) that to be thir job? _____ has not required a
passkey ~~being~~ ^(that one is thereby) not not not a person. perhaps one does not
not want to be found   unsupple in the main and unduly hided
                        that one ys most of all (the time) w/ oneself

lovers reversed: dump hunk

what you hold is what you will be-hold
fish or flesh
flesh or fleece
but not both
you wdnt just glean
the gutted pig flies from the middens
and grind them into a gelatinous goo
for your sustenance
and yet you live   and breathe the upper air
nor yet lie gulletted   in the cruel shallows?
your face is pressed against the glass of a crowded restaurant
you gnaw a hunk of cheese
hookups fall thru
you dont know what it's like
to be treated nice
s/o wd rather stay closeted than date you
straight and queer people of all stripes
are a little repelled but mostly indifferent to you
nothings working
not that sigil   nor the online dating,
the serious kind and the sex kind
nor craigslist, that last moorings of the desperate

notes from the mummy chamber

Inuksuk: 'like a person' (Inuktitut)

I will not sit within their fishtraps
w/ rudimentary arms
and kohl stained cheeks
from simulated tears

as clouds do, streaking across the black sea
bound gazelle
trussed goose
the whole recumbent upon a single moccasin

plagued by lotuses
the fishes of horus
strain for breath
while foxes praise the gooseshooter

their faïence upraised as cowhorns
grasping for the sundisk
a human with no wings
but a bird for a face

what flaubert never saw
hygrometed pots of unguents
or whoso buries or tucks their wish
into the fat folds of the pharaohs neck

the rabbit & the crow

all of our psychological problems manifest in our writing
my advisor, a linguist, and my best friend, a psychologist, agree
what do you get when a compass breaks
an hour inopportune
cree rabbitstep or texas twostep
lead with the left and count to four
the dog is turning in circles, it is preparing to die
ghost dance
w/ its insurgent meter
made up as medicine
for when the sweat of your ass precludes your wisdom
frog dance, fish dance, taino snake dance, crow hop
you leap nimbly across the coals, nevermind that you
have wings and cd fly away at any time
wind blew through & the cowboys went under
whoosh—bam
shot and shot thru

who is not yr cousin?

bears may be brutal
but they never did n/t
to bruise up the earth

& englyssh is so filled
w/ periphrasis
metal band seeks bassist

in which one searches
amerikka backward: akkirema
I pay money for money

who holds up thir
coffee by way of
hailing a taxi

for pigeon read rock dove
jobs that fell thru
say goodbye to the grouper forever

who therwithal
—palm and pine—
r so thoroly discomfitted

what's eating hildegard?

they locked up all the deodorants at the pharmacy
so much for my spicy sculpture

I'm melting down the mounds of greeze
into a thickish soup
for your pleasure,

but I'm having a problem
I like you but I'm the creepy older person
& my offerings of tea & chocolates are not platonic
evry word doth almost tell it—

the one-fingered typist
and the halfmoon network, myn oracle
are all along the mizzenmast w/ my louche aspect

my friends, I have broken with you
& with the iambic forever
there will be no re-calling me
where I'm headed

burglar who forgot to loggoff thir
f***book page

crème-de-mer you cant
extinguish a fire, and expect it to keep
on burning

ack, buttery

that one is not always (not)
                          disconsolate
how that one treats (mistreats) th'other

being obvious at whatever one is—the judeity, the genera,
that I make (of myself) a cheapness. its hyde unlissomish. a field
peopled w/ concrete nouns—obviate unicorns toying w/ chiffon.

          the dism(antled) subject, myn ejaculate,
the swallowed snot
          the nature of desire is that it orrsteps

and (be sure if you do to fall) well.
          to where one can become cumbered
the pen vibrated before one's profferred back pocket,

(here) one was unrevoked by thir appreciation
of poirot's moustaches. that actually they coveted it to the point
of injecting themself w/ medicines.

wherr the point (of privvacy) ends
thinking I will look up and see yew
somewhen soon

the beast what enwrenched
gobbets in toto
out the whale's maw

what do they know of suffering,
who eat of pineapples yearround

Lrsn, brute battlements of infamy cd not
nor the former planet pluto, nor those
pulchritudinous characters who scape
even usen's reach, the plumes, nor yet
those fruits who are bred to be
of uniform size, watermelons squard
compliant papayas, I followed the norteñəs
train to train, the field populates or the field
was filled—what do they know of suffering
who eat of pineapples yearround?
& the edifices tho they enscrape the sky
were not so near as high as we
down by that ridiculous stream,
whos dappled mere the better part of me
but if we make this our last moorings
it were no burthen to me, friend
who attend yr company this day

like w/ like wars not

The ocelots with their mathematical faces.
—NATALIE DIAZ, 'It Was the Animals'

th'harmonious shrinkage of the serpent in face of angels
who goeth wayfully in the mud up to thir nostrills
marveliss monandis 'isánáklésh
face half-stained with minerals
and hartely (this embrigature) goes sally-ho forth
to proclaim thir lineage ligned
w/ romanz-reading-on-the-boke?

curt happenstance in tyme
much as one is marvelld at
is kickd therew/all out the library
unfaithfully early tiraloo
twas s/t to imprint upon
as a woodcut or a charcoal stick

feeding on that slothfuller flame, that goeth not
midst flames but rather treats
of heretickes most onerous (having been——
therefor to have companye) amongst
fellawes, having been flayed (helas)
in full view that courteous messenger

who, upraised for thir light habitat
and thir supposedly high ingenium
made one to feel inferior amid the flames
and therefor has one not made oneself the fool?
doubly, triply immured in the pneumatics?

like with like wars not, joy delights in joy
but think not the cormorant once
redolent any less airworthy, whose
minutest adulations temper my goings

—

'Isánáklésh: Apache deity, earth mother, wise woman adorned with white clay

irreversibly like apples

irreversably like appels, the stones of an age
drip obliquely into your woolen mout
no beclouded crystals they
confine themselves to finer form
the precipice of arepa   leffaloes
peak of an ark   cut rubyes

when will springtime come on in

when will springtime come on in   ta-la tala tala
winters gonna do me in   ta-la talaa tala

we go as the crow flies
to the pines
where we are free
but ever watched and ever watchful
when will springtime come on in   ta-la tala tala
winters gonna do me in   ta-la talaa tala

we go as the crow
to the pines where berries grow   tala tala tala

on branch of pine
we snatch at them
w/ paw and maw
we eat the tender grasslets   tala tala tala

only to puke them up
on the soft moss
or later on the kitchen floor
when will springtime come in   ta-la tala tala
winters gonna do me in   ta-la talaa tala

as the crow will fly
we go to the pines

to chase the sticks
& chew the grasses
when will springtime come on in   ta-la tala tala
winters gonna do me in   ta-la talaa tala

as we lean us on a bough
as we betake us up the stair
when will springtime come on in   ta-la tala tala
winters gonna do me in   ta-la talaa tala
when will springtime finely come   ta-la tala talaa
by the pawing of my thumb   ta-la talaa tala

# of mongrelitude

A bed of roses itself is no bed of roses. Nobody wants an e-book, they would
sooner leave you in the lake, a den of mouldering slime for your coffin. Everbody
calling it a recession—theyr in a delusion. I am privy to these contradictory sit-
uations where I am told first the one and then the other bathroom is the wrong
one. Madame, c'est là! and then o monsieur! je me suis tromper! If I powder my
nose in the tudes, if I choose to walk barefoot in the small hours . . . you yourself
are a healing property you know. You came home from the fair only to join the
circus its festal moods, to feast on frost. So one learns to make thir way amid the
multitudes. And know bliss as a cowperson.

I know I am the small fry here. Whose harnassed thot drove winter aback, gos
wrastlin thir daemon underground. Tho the stirrups brinked and tha mud was
broke, I looked down to the rivulet between the tracks, and couldnt tell if what I
saw was a turd or twisted rust metal. & the rats, rooting amid the black death and
the typhus. One comes out steppin, their eyes fallen on the shores, cognizant only
to the trash they mucked around. Suddenly you and your neighbors thighs are
pressed together, accidental camaraderie or blunt eroticism. And neither of you
move away.

We race toward the mounds of gravel, the morning star met with its wanderer.

dog on dog aggression

who are innit for pure fame
tho art magicked like newcomers
when the canary come stumping
in the coalmine

—noteworthy the gimmick
to apprehend any traveler
bound by thir headlamp
but w/o thir bearing
schlonged into the farreaching atmosphere—

who—frekisshe—envyes the gesture
mislaid upon the cheek
one cometh saying
my mutual interests are different from yrs

xavier—once hilt
thanatos wuz demure
nor was there any meat in thir manner
nor do they mete out punishment

θanatos
whan grey
bespecks
ppl & thir devices
s/time a dog peeping out its basket

I am having trouble connecting
w/ my constituents
the arkitects little imagynd
how their work would be undone

hell and gore

as a range ferry
this time coagulates
even on the verge of nonsense
embroiders a fine hope w/o a subject
of the several possible recipients
not one will do
orangerie
shut down for the season
but the old oaks
scent of a musky forrest mistaken for an incense
dreamt my therapist was leaving me
even in the midst of my confession
I'd never seen a moon
so neatly cut in half
or birches
w/ their tops lopped off
they say when the bullet hit the brain
of the swedish king charles XII
it was like the sound of two fingers
slapping the palm [thwack]
maskarnas liv—life of worms
when I wanted you
to see my error, trust me
I'd just unhook my garment
my sadness wasn't as exquisite as I thought
the oaks

misshape themselves
to follow the flock
4-leggèds, steamy-breathds
sun sun sun worship
sháa sháa sháa sháa
amenable dung
o may it
claypainted personparent
a feather on a twig on a branch on a tree
consider my exquisite error
as a lapsed torture
sometimes a life of worms
proves candelabrious
adumbriated

sometimes I feel like
I'm the tool of the devil

tobreke! the glut in tyranny,
to ramshackld the bête in thir own bêtise
noo Im had en*uf* to be tribbald w/
itself one brestless n peced self togedre
really, it shd go away in a tansy
feelings cum reeflings arise in the tisane

oceanic feeling

pope become pilgrim
as manatee become
the master. lived w/ the person
for many years and never knew them, etc.
humanized mouse
whos liver is anthropic
venticular
not like the seat of my desire
which had bright eyes
and peers at me thru the gutter
nothin but horseglue and sentiment
pony sliders
canter no more
by the time a certain spectre
had enterred the air by the
time a certain atmosphere therefrom
the ayre
crow hopped over
then its handle
(s)hewed
resolved itself into a plastic bag

some say an army
of horsepeople

some say an army of horsepeople
some say soon the handle wull fly right off
only to be ambiguated by a single letter

who hath bespoke
wheelis   flyan upright
who sat bolt upright in thir coffin

look it's victor hugo
the great poet
talking to chopin

who hath commandeered all tusks
only the particulate matter
the very follicles

yeh I have to leave you
alone and give you
your mouth back

the godawfullest thing
on this bleak earth
some say an army of horsepeople
but I say it's—

what wuz therr izzaye?

whose gait is unhurried.
—AL-ḤUSAYN IBN AḤMAD IBN KHĀLAWAYH, *Names of the Lion*
(TRANS. DAVID LARSEN)

if whatt there was to recordd in me was suhthing in me

the fallout IZZAYE

are only inordinary
one has the secret craving one cannat get enough

erp, epps—r not producing t but suhthing is

who has the luxury of a slow pace
in face of foes

yes, even further
apace in the industrial landscape

never nas non
never will n-n-n-no-thing be enuf

red sky at morn

tho what hath been primordial—thir fronte, ofttimes in geste, as in ACCORDANCE
they hath pronomounced themself (most onerous) who forsaw (midst all lord-
lyngs) the hairy belly upraiseth itself from the sepulchre studded w/ flames—that
this geste was made hereabouts / one amends thir own selfe not a priori the lover
but in the act of *transing*—that's what their therapist called it—does not one some-
times *arrive* or end-to-begin? yes DEATH but of a spirit also which goeth nat w/
fleshy mouldings, haha, not w/ *that guy* anyway.

tho the rivulets be finite, the tokens are talking

who yet lacks urbanitas
but whos tribes
very soon undeceived
palmy somaticism
toxic to the billions nay
to tha hundreds

tha fore
to tha fore
     hath scraped
neptitude forth n whether rightly
no ahl nawtbe cxld
kickselld
who speaks ceaselessly

whose gringitude outswung thir pores
bent over onna desk

may wear the kerchief in a certain pocket
but the military awready fucken them in the ass

who must attch thir ear to the cell the
moment the train upsurgeth the tunnell

half agin as much
longfoot sioux
whos several distress
layall misshappen

but who manages to mock the pain away
daub thir way btwn raindrops

in all queer excesses, surriously
whoso lounges
a duvet upon

automat metropolis

FOR ERICA LEWIS

it seemed like a holy place / we could sing right outloud / the things we could
not say / pray with me over the phone / close your eyes / and swallow the sun.
—ERICA LEWIS, 'and I am you*' *as

check it, princez
at 1 w/ the automat
(arrogance) stood 1-fer-2

per the navigant oratist
—then check me on sunday,
whined the orifice

são paulo metropolis
double the width of L.A.
the verticality of manahatta

pales against
million degrees diesel amazonia
stereo concret
casa das rosas
annihalates
whos dominant glosseur

who hath come unto weerat
prolaclaiming xir mode

sleeping bty
meerkat oddity

truly bahia
hath captured buena sera
quem evocas la bahia
negras comos gli clouds
parense ojo

not that þat hath nereth into naught
habitat aspect est blood
west coast yall, yes yes yall

ghanì 'ntų'í dìníìhįį killer-of-enemies
bequieted the bear
whos scratches made the waters we row upon
I drink the therraflu romantic comedy
I think all landings are hoaxes

melancholy lake

who never thinks too cold, too coldly of themself
who lay awake (toûtseul) in tha dark room & thot to
    disappear themself.
who would <u>not</u> (not not notnot) be consoled & raged
on pompous ponces, jowlyfacd rich people &
    that melancholic pool, despair

last night I dreamt brad pitt and I were lovers, we
    had each committed a murder and confessed to
    ours in turn—he had killed someone who wouldn't
    leave w/ him right away to go somewhere, a party
    or something. I—I had killed someone just then,
    as we took a turn around melancholy lake, which
    at first (in the dream) was a salt mine. the salt
    farmer was giving a lecture on the ecology of
    the pool, it was in santa cruz, it was toxic, (we do
    not anymore hear of a clean pool or pond)
    (so that even narcissus is uglified) there were chunks
    of it, salt, floating about at the edges of a pool or
    pond, resembling ice. I could not (cannot) recollect
    the details of my own murder (the one I had
    myself $^{(myself)}$ committed$_{of\ late}$). $^{in\ any\ case,}$we walked around the lake
(as I said) on a vertiginous & slippery path of
salt which seemed like ice, and the ^{broken}pieces of it floating near, salt rather, gave
a cold and melancholic feeling, and the color of the blue of the pool turned

pale green at its center, making it appear warm
and tropical. the whole effect was so seductive
brad wanted to leap in. I understand, I communicated
to him, the desire to leap into the lake of despair but
come now old boy do let's carry on

involuntarily I licked my lips

rusty rivulate
    undulata
        —the folio
           brink ottomat—oddity

only a forearm
involuntarily I licked my lips
so few people are well-formed
  (formosa)

où es tu
quel chemin
a tu pris

a mallet and a ratchet
seductively undulating

pelican of orchards
paramox

who merits thir mask
but not thir grey hairs

grizlar bears
be poppin
dommage in pericular

ones owen scope
ta be bridled

paramatrest
binite   adjaçon

if only there were a
glory for that hole

if only there were a glory for that hole
helas but the flume does nat arise
in tandem wit myn owen
th'amnesiac bilt for dirty laundry
wher all ones blotted lines came back to haunt
commiserating for weeks in the muck w/ the grains and grainules
to have not forgone ones ancestors
to have rilly meant what one said
to have earlier been one way and then an other w/o contradiction
above all to have not playd ones friends false

fried-eyed /
banned poetry words

it's not the russian it's the wu-tang crushin
—WU-TANG CLAN

slip up and get creped like suzette
travelong to thir erstwhal milieu
steeped in toxins
ever flushing xem out
along the crick the fried fishlings foam
and soak thir minor manticores
battered eyeballs batting at yew

the way the waves in the painting curve
so many telltale infernal tickings
I knew I had to stop writing nonsense.
jack spicer laffed and laffd.
but arturo desimone wasnt laffing at me
and brenda iijima definitely wasnt fucking laughing.

and I used a poem w/ all the banned poetry words, <u>poetry</u>, <u>angels</u>,
<u>filament</u> (fear of saying 'thread'), <u>aperture</u> (fear of saying 'hole'),
<u>rococco</u>, <u>chiaroscuro</u>
especially fucking *aperture*, most banned poetry word.
and there are more I reckon: thighs, language, the phrase 'the body' (it's the the
that does me in, Michael says), gossamer, affected use of overpronounced Spanish

in otherwise English-language writing, pearl, pause, breath, anything French, liminal, palimpsest, I, ghosts, souls, beams when used of eyes, azure when applied to sea or sky, any 'poetic' terms such as 'neath, tungsten, thrumming, esoteric plant names, references to fantastical places like Arcadia, also 'tween and o'er, sand, Greek or Roman god names, desire . . . yr . . . instance, espejo, gaze, MYSTICAL, Dear, 'To Spicer,' banned, gunmetal, all tree names, beyond, erotic, lone, single, all adverbs, we, word/world, hoarfrost, cheesecloth, any nouns made into verbs, ostensibly, matrix, kitsch, sediment, essence, 'architecture of,' 'the social,' mist, floating, moist especially in the context of a 'moist night' or evening, typically any penis, erection, nipple words, eternal, death, quiche; scry, limn, lapidary, sidereal—not banned but groan-worthy—shard, salt, luminous, the phrase 'in my mind' . . .

how obvious

I just noticed there aren't nearly so many errors in speech as in writing . . . one never knows how obvious they're being. Person singing thir bloody guts out, los autobuses 'shuttle,' pocketcalls the impossible dream, would not could not cotton to that sort of thing. Old person painting thir nails pink on the subway, who knows precisely what an adolescent I am. Last glimpse of the water at Jersey . . . well if death will not behave! whose embrigature (natch) went bolting

like a well worn cuff
parcells of snout
small yield of peas
platonic friendship who
treat therapy like gossip
utter illusio of privvacy

was not the roofdeck a paradise?
replacing the KY hat on the drunk man?

on such a nite did young Lorenzo etc.
a princez what escapd hir handlers
against this fruity little score
for the halcyon interval owed hir

all those desperate little gnats plastered to the window by the lamp
a griggle left on the tree

abreast the linda lou
32nd largest yacht in amerikka
day-after-day w/ their
gay spouses

in clover w/ those creatures
like bleeding cobwebs they were
who shut the lid on their finer feelings
to end their days in neptune's arms

blathersum

as holds such hostelryes aback
markem made a face
w/ the opposite of shadows
all the way glimpsingly thru the bridge
(thatt one) twinkd w/ portraittture
wanted to spit
grew a beard
betook itself to the crowd
n en face those sundry multitudes
clove fast to the hyphe

despite of space

sely rat, sely rat
I cd not court yr likeness back

if only a horizon wd present itself—
a razor to the face

with your help I hope to acquire a meal
—despite of space

the legless one
to the person who jettisons leftovers

yes Im sent on a fools errand
petulant skoler

wrongeyed thinkerr
why the fly think it ok

to sit on my knee
phantasiestücke

yr beauty is dissipating as you type
it fronts but it ys a geste

xe is nat merely to be won over
w/ kissing noises

lyric cd be prowes
a cricket on a heap of trash

(wot my blood grows)
wherrwolfian, coodepoo

the fly wot sits on its own murder weapon
who dont want s/t prayrishe

el toro partido
the bull in parts

for our meeting on the loam:

I will not persist under this sack of weeds
        most fearsome gambit to withhold

nor invest in the porkish veneer
        of stoploss   —one became so serious and hard—in the donut shop

a drunk flipping the pinball machine
        nostrils flaring, a shady bizniss

suns uprising

                        bunnyboy seething

perhaps it is a force against my fine affacement
        perhaps—in my enthusiasm—

flankd by what
        junior compass

nor revell to that effect
nor cant to the porcine dream

helen, source of death

AFTER XENAKIS

orestian movement
wherr the sevral stringd lyre

poor cassandra
provoked into a false falsetto
its pinky-plectrum
greekish-cum-cali

waved our silver flags
w/ the angels in the aisles

who made thir debut
demoored to thundrous applause
thir own sanguine ymage
accentless in the barrage—fearing
to controvert—none—'is not a snob [one] swears'

n/a applicable
one failed by thir own
sweet measure, tries not to
smile lewedly into the light

breaches ones owen
erstwhal abode (one's)
complete unloveliness
yet we slavered after it

sympathy butters no parsnips

great speckled bird who
prayed when it played
just off from 440
aquila chrysaetos golden eagle
over new mexico

was it deth to dele
that I stood apart from myself
apparently only to see——

the chaparral motel
changed and unchanged
flesh and fleece
monopulate the clovers

had the sound of being flung
like an ampule popped
or poprocks dropped
the gays called it poppers
martichaud called it vers libre

did you ever see a robin weep
when leaves dont turn right
the leaves so that
they dont know how to turn right
birds in wrong states

sympathy butters no parsnips
too bad craft said otherwise
whod rage and consider it a labor
it's worse to know I got myself here
thru my own choices and apparent desires
D. said she thought she was 'witnessing a torment'
of me beside myself

pressing my thumb to my palm
to achieve lucidity in dreams
it was alrite as a conceit
it did a little bow for the muppets in the upper pew
who, cackling, hauled their boat onto the spurious ice

chaparral character

for thinking that my Love could hold a love
how my enterprise alas
forwent a parasol
now only in purgatory
pens going dry
sweet adeline keeps slipping off the network
how much time did I spend in the æther
each keystroke lorded over by big-lover-sibling
the muchness of my avatar
      this fallow chaparral character
ever-present in the de-characterization
severe prolongued drought
then ill-equipped to handle rain
      furious at my love, being furioused at,
ferocity crested. antipathy. bon ami in the bath.
veered to arise as a tendency in plants to consciousness
my pineal gland   glamored by sunrize
hastily it forbore to make a joke
it soldered thinking it
stood straight   face upright to the sun
unlike the thinker
pondering over its toilet
or the scholar
gaze cast downward at a book
or was it chaparral in character

whethersoever it were
(marry to be humanlike)

hands rush away from life / toward stoves / even concrete drains wish to be human
—TONGO EISEN-MARTIN

marry to be humanlike
birds eat planes
and the 4 sqr of whitail
deer go unmounted

kóshkeya
enemigma
an eve-enning emma
elk and

since anon could be all like
right therr in the room
with you

someone is banging a cowbell
on whut my mynde
on whut my hyde

in a narrow eros
we herr humbly
—that which ys—
—'   '—

eat dirt, oasis, myn oracle

far: not to be sure
la: the garishness of violets
persisting in the assumption of raindrops

the small rain down can rain
the small rain veritably down can rain
way hiya way hiya way hiya
way hiya way hiya

in a narrow eros
we herr humbly

far: the snatched oasis
that which is—
—'   '—
whenever I'm away from you
I always get these lovesick blues

flowr bows down thir head—
we're innit
herr vanquished
eat dirt, oasis,
myn oracle

gon aerial wolfhuntin

beganne to be of the milieu
tha bluefurrd devil then seized on
whan to besmirch even the alpine
sediment goes wolfhuntin, adieu—
wrench thir erstwhile barrell from them
erupt it into a fine brine—drill-drill! powpow!

widdershins

clever litle conundrum
what ys onlie somwhat alive

no-one of no-place
and therrafter the sutures

whan bitches play at faggotry
contrario modo

a fascinare
precluding blowholes

as do bloodspurts
irrationality

myrmidons' transfixity
irascible as ants

natur bi
or trifurcated

fain I wd tie me to
illa juventius þt ys so nice

the parson interjected you *can*
but you *may not*

ambivalence becometh

lo the hartslung moon
peeks lewdly out tha cloud

twinlite of the towrs
runs rampant in my mouth

myn entourage whut
cometh to me in folds, in the fields

endurrs heavy scarring
as thir mind hesitates

you dont need to get
fuckd up to see visions

you cant underestimate a gymnast's start-value
dalí presenting harpo w/ a barbed wire harp

cmon shawn
cmon winchester

errborn has been lying to us
a lack of willingness if you will

zukofsky reciting hiawatha
in yiddish on a lower eastside streetcorner

artur schnabel doing bach
lipan apache singing in lakota

of all the bill and coo
that makes es wooing parlous

who swindle a soup
divers' showers and thir shammies

one star in thir square
of skye

amador you dont need
to get fuckd up to see visions

on antony and cleo

I'll never see't! for I am sure mine nails / Are stronger than mine eyes.
—WILLIAM SHAKESPEARE, *Antony and Cleopatra*, 5.2.224–5
(Cleo's maidservant Iras, on not wanting to see Cleo lead in a triumph)

s/t the creek of Octavius is all forlorn
& I triumvirated
w/out so much as the trunk
of my throte ys all forworn
I go n get
pyramises, drunken
plural of pyramids

o fill me till the cup be hid
trick us out w/ cypress
annoint thy sauce
to a further alcatraz of the hart

thabsence of a white
star on a horses head
was thot t'impair
its value

cleo
bombards the messenger
fears the cups harried
what they call maudlin I call
magdalayna

hallo to you that do
bow b4 cupid's courte who
do hym mickel much desport
I trow you never
come up short

fish n chips
cuirassier

flesh was evermore a
sonnetto
and no salty savor
plumbs the lack

not the sloppy religiosity

For you, love, I brake my glass, / Your gown is furred with blue.
—ANON. (mid-16th century)*

nore yet the doggy religiosity
nor the backyard heat
hives erupt from ones furr
who pusses in measures

ad instantitem tanto
and brittany vie for the meat
erupting from the vma curr
what upcurls from that same foam

---

*Part of a lyric originally printed in Richard Kele's *Christmas carolles newely Inprinted*, probably between 1546 and 1552, according to P. Bliss. It also appears in *Biographical Miscellanies*, ed. Bliss, 1813.

the tabloids are filled w/ mancrush and bromance

limpet
dodging the hue and fie

now I cheep
starlight ~~fawl~~ fahl

      banks unstung

the tabloids are filled
with mancrush and bromance

we're splitting before the bad
jellies roll into town

tevs man
wotever dont see the stink dont thwart it

when the water gets
sleazy in august

the myth of the subway

funnyface barbers, us
wimp become hunk
omi the tanline
turtle inna pneumatic tube
engorging softserve snowlilies
coney island bound Q train
rats rush the copper platform

efficiency module in liberty city
cop syndicate w/ hunk output
I'm paranoid, but not paranoid enough
eyes in the pigeons, eyes in the trees

camras surround th'mayoral compound
we stuff our face w/ watercress
exclusive to our paranoia

fed up w/ its own cappadry
extinctifying the honeycomb
w/ crapshoot cavalry
and bare minimum LED

the uselessness of
magicking death

FOR RO WRIGHT

I'm a threefacd dawg in the yard,
bare of ballast
onna windowseat in the mews

the truth is that xe loves to gossip
esp. w/ a gossip who has good gossip
but they must keep their gossipping on the DL

if only I had sent those photographs
you wdnt be smashd on your bicycle

poem for r having left new york

dear mozart I too want
what napoleon did for etruria
earned or unearned
and I consider u one of my dearest friends

brkln is defaced w/ memories
wherr the whites displaced the jews
one is kowtowing @ its edges
b-rock boyking w/ a bad A—
was that all I could think to say of daffodils?

going haywire in a golden haybasket
tonite the fog is like san francisco
only not so lowdown
I want to put it in my throat
salieri wd cant himself seedily
find them submerged in the underdeeps
to see how subway ppl live

s/time one is lonely
in the firmament
one has n/t but never enuf time
no I cant have coffee
no I dont want to look at yr screenplay

+tumult

the lark is . . . inelegant but xe is outside the city
one tries not to refer to the one
the subway driver split the limbs
n brakes n squeaks n speeds
at recordcount decibels
unlike bart, which is run by robots
how teary stein lukkd outside the library
crouchd like a buddha among the pansies

poem for shorty courtier

there's nothing like bread for a gentleone's bowing
some have the love of an antifog fello
some serendipitously curtsy
some—rancrous w/ shapely gams and natty garmentry
do scoff and skirt the crickery masses

once hyacinthine, now pert
was that all I could think to say of daffodills?
merely a crickateer in the scrum,
or a profiteer hazing stricture?

rules for bones

are you sure yr a person
you look more like an artichoke
if even the parabolist has thir purpose
if even the tipi poles r famous

broccolini for nonce-coolery
adjacent mulberry
to sissy beanpods
& git-along-little-dogies
parlous petracitours
most lazy susans
and picpoul cannabis

we playd bones w/ popish miniatures
xe had me weigh platinum in my palm
I was like got weed
who first kissd my hand, then yrs
until you ride yr own train yr open

rolfings alternate name:
structural integration
tijuana boxcarstyle
rules for bones

or pause to gaze on the moody chest of spartacus

garbage juice everywhere
OTC tequila, non pareil they are
w/o equal
or pause to gaze on the
muddy chest of
spartacus
its blu eye

causeth me to lean
despondently out tha window

who speke depe
tunnelis
twice as like to pour the tea

I greatly prefer under my paws
the paving stones

who have harborid no
illusions
whos twetes enflict

—yonder comes my mastre—

a bee's feather

in pleasure as wot makes raquet
to whit our own racketeering
makes monstrous cry—noteworthy of thirself
one capitulates—pourquoi ma fee or feess
so impertinent as to produce a map
—w/o wearing a wig—

one's meercoat—inreverse
the trial (or tha) troll of hey nonny nonny
semenaunt en fábula
too blaut to be bonny
—as if I minded my own judiciary—!
    xanadu   politico   frijolillo   myn eye
molts on the untidy passage
of a bee's feather. bosh!
there never was any adjudicated form of aerial travel
to spurt ducements on. that one most humbly deranges and belabors.

I am not supposed—supposed by others—to
be telling the bees—& yet wot's monstrous?!

the glorious bêtise
         of the chickpea
involuntarily brot into thymage
    non euclidean
    non aristotelian
    non newtonian

                                    one's mouse
(trolly lolly) on its lone (therefore have)
heart. cor, one has thir own fish ta fry.
the unicornity of bodie. thir rages.
              once it showed me a kindness

manytimes a fleece to get punky by
              to flesh all & have a good row
how one expresses so n so (a feeling)
              erst—once't—a double tome
togedre & en face the great haunt
they gargle in euclyptian tidewater
heady toyles assailed
              one presses—agaynst tha mark
just reads thir toes for to-day.

as one eaglescout to an other
one's afeard to stele out in the hall
manytimes a farce has been held
(and maintaind) theyr not tafault
onlyeye the swartness of the smythes
brennwaterys
thir avunction
if only to discombobulate limbage

lawd—my tailor – ------------------------------ -   — -
aslape but for the droning fly
who is this wertheim?
& wherr goes my slip if not in the pneumatics?

great tidewater, a brade, a blaut my thinking
(nor noghte) avunctuary

in which I've not not taken part
heavy my city! and o! my limbic
assoils—I have not the hrt
—whose proper huts bewail—
& the fwoosh of the rail mistook for a tide
where one's hamhocks r a daily beast

howd I alite here—ta this place
whan one is of a terrain: most upwardly
most awkward? ahm I so brent?
daft as to require an erbe?

is one afterall to remain chaste? aye in thir
comforts? to what remains, in wot niddling thorofare?
here habitat. here here perspicacious.
        —made explycit
        hollyhockd   midst rogues
one brays to filth.

now one speaks of a privy most onerous
that they pipe in the sound of crickets (or is that a distant alarm racketting?)
heywot? donchudelay???? em disrobing emself in the dawn,
the table w/ its owen scalloped edge
far rockaway . . . legends of irelaunde . . .
fleur unfaced. better the pyp is not permanaunt.

airroir

But aren't we just splinters of stars?
——NORMA COLE, *14000 Facts*

heliosnoop
one takes the tack
scatters and who remains
solja do you sip
fucka you suck
if they unzip?
o but this chaînes are bloody
& we ner abide
in your choice of an opaque finish
arent we all just shards
of some forsaken star
whos coffin meanwhile
disgust me, tree heavy with ginkgo
norma saying, 'even the sun has cancer'
do I look like a loser
arent we all just shards
of some vary particulate garter
bereft of an adoring moon
bleepd of eternal darnation
what fools beknownst

make us all homosexuals,
o muse, o privy muse

yew are a forestt in a tree, unpro
saical and crass-in-philosophie.
moreover there is—
that those trees are tending to—
I would be unprosaic too, if it werent for all
those creatures struggling in a heap of trash—!
lest you flirt and forget to do the work
of a would-be polymath. a sensitive
inattendant to the newly dead
what want rescue.
whos lies are a force against my fine
effacement
in an aqueerium of angry fish. one is
a movement that has lost its relevance
by force, by collumnar force.
I come to this city & I swear,
I swear I am not like dorothy, I already
knew the seat of my desire. I hoarded
planetary secrets like a spy: one privy
room has another scented soap than
another. it smells like pine, winter and flannel. that
one person is from a certain planet, and another
is from another, grant no further.
why shd some not smell of pine and birch,
or sum of dayes-eyes?
make us all homosexuals,
o tridented muse, o privy muse.

fowles in tha frith

after 'Fowles in the frith' (MS Douce 139, f. 5r), late 13th century

fowles in þe frith
þe fisses in þe flod
and i mon waxe wod
much sorwe i walke with
for beste of bon and blod

turkey in the straw
fishes in my maw
and I moan tooroola
much melancholie I make
for that beastss sake

turkey in tha straw
fishes in tha pond
& I upflay its maw
wot moanings I make
for a bloody bestiary

doves are in the elm
bambi in the sea
and ahm mad crazy
iron sorrow iz my wroth
devil amid dayeseyes

foaming in the piss
fishes in the midst
and I troll merrily—
taloo talay
fa tooril toorel toolay

imaginary and actual koalas, troly loly

the tong wot ranges
similia similibus
the flameater eats
of the flamethrowers flames

s/how candid wit
overall plaisance
imaginary koalas and
creepy quakers

turning hoary is only
as wild is troly
living for nonce is
the creed of the ponces

dipping a pigtail in the inkwell
s/time it's just sentiment
myope because
they fixate on the boke

whyfore doth that grome
go wandering along the scrim
philip among the leaves
still a desideratum

the several smitty
& unfortunat blancheflour
r tha bizniss
tho art magicked like newcomers

Dis pure diss

FOR BRYN KELLY

to see the shape of your spectacles in the sky
which overarches our conception of ourselves
too big feet, weird voice, flat affect
gives way to a rounder orb
like and unlike you
cleave to me
your nostalgia is your salvation
a placenta they say
is the only organ you grow as an adult
ugh
bear w/ me
except for the skin
the extra cells around our inks and scars
the very bird you winged in upon
dont go dark on me
have on this
bridge of bathetic sighs
a chicken for every bird 'doing' pot
may it haunt their houses plesantly
when the feelings come, after the initial numbness,
they are gormless, relentless, causing amazement
I went to the woodshed freshly smoked to write this gospel song for you
a guy yells at me
stick it in your eye!

on treasure island tammy says
the janitor rules everything
perhaps you would be satisfied
with a mind less nimble than your own
and francis the albino porcupine
directs our gaze toward san francisco
where I left my pick and shovel
you fit more livin
in a pinhead than I cd hope to haunt granada
trite as a periscope w/ the gain turned up to 8
when you mashed up the
blood and the cum and the lamb, singing shady grove,
tight like a narwhal knows nirvana at the gates
Dis pure diss

we birds

FOR EVAN KENNEDY

. . . senseless metiers . . . my welcome into a kind of gaggle, if you birds will.
—EVAN KENNEDY

I open my unfit beak.
—DAWN LUNDY MARTIN

the first false spring is here
the dirty snow is melting
we birds
arch our neck for the worm
believe in turning a blind eye to get it
we molted too soon
spring was receding ever as it tempted us
to deal in cryptocurrencies
& mt. gox is bust

we birds fly into
the orange sky illumined
against the gray flash above the marcy st. projects
—little one breaks flock—
how long do I have to stay in character

the sun—finally—bore no resemblance
to the one who floated before us all asteam with moxie

the last time a human stood, nose quivering
against the scene of devastation

a firetruck whose wheels spin out
profesh-grade portraits that speak in fish language
who can distinguish between civil, nautical
and astronomical twilight

I, rockdove, I, seagull, rat of the sky
worm winged like an eagle
am told I am getting
more of everything
more cake
more worms
more orifices and things to go in the orifices

two horses succeed where the truck failed
despite their clumsiness and their face blindness
I lost my fortune to the wild boar what gored me
I pressed my eye to the keyhole and fell away
the scientist was pointing to the tell-tale snow leopard scat
saying 'from my own species-perspective, I salute you'

aren't we all just worms in the wind
trying to stick ourselves to a branch?
'you'll know it's cold when the mountains turn blue'
lizard that looks like a dandelion
beatle that looks like a rock
whos skill in catching fishes
like water off a duck's back,
only a bear   in the river   shaking its coat

bear with a fondness for fishes
bird with a fondness for crabcakes
river that flows both ways

painful rube in the shallows
don't know how to smoke fuck drink
eventually was made to eat the meat

Shakespeare had a sovereign not a sister
I said to the dog, you're every creature
and-if-the-stars-do-seem-in-night-to-prate
who prefers the springy grass to the salted concrete

we birds go down to the milky river,
between the ochre cliffs
knowing life depends on the consumption of bodies by other bodies
an arm or a channel or a valley reveals itself
parched begonia
long suffering aloe
to top it off, it was the end times
one bird called it 'la grim de la grim'

candles were conveyed
—mm placed—as if a gift
gazelle-predator
predator-gazelle
a snow leopard in snow
the whole thing was a mare's nest
students place classes in a 'shopping cart'

now it was a drone
now it was a gnome

that sat itself on a rock
that cd disappear itself at will
that seemed to dispense wisdom

saying things like, 'picture a collie
made entirely of melons—
melon-collie'
the face, the face of the one that took your meds

I love not snow leopards the less
but birds more
converted into aversion
converted into a version

march is by turns a lionish lamb, a lambish lion
uncouple us from our crime
where castles are horses
objects for fire or war
kiss us on our split lip, our bloody snout, our bent beak
something wicked this way comes
books will be made of oblong coal
styluses of liquid metal

I know what the story is supposed to be
and supposedly my place innit
by the time it was not supposed to have mattered
I had given up my crumpet
and the creature that climbs on the high crags
something-saint-mary

nor will we use technology
nor will we hook up from where we're sitted ten feet

across from each other
who is the creature itself and not its avatar, at least for now
the mountaintops don't flinch
as the avalanche gets going

we birds do not pluck at the
cakes given to osiris
on that eastern side of the narrows
whos hair was thought to be made of lapis

in the end, we all had to eat worms
in the end, all we had to eat—was worms
in the end, we all had worms to eat

the death of script

I can't go kicking this rusty blade no further
we can all name ourselves smurves
when the terrors of modernity seem quaint
plash of water
monumental tree trail
tripple faggot
only god xemself
short buff gay
agog in 8 ft waves
of totally tubular efflorescence
remembers those empassioned tweets
on the theme of cursive handwriting

as the owl augurs

FOR INÉS TALAMANTEZ

I have an hour to read marcabru and fall in love
to study the medicines and put a rock in each corner of the house
and pray over it with pollen as my elder advised
to test my unextraordinary knowledgeses
to briefly wonder whether I was actually under a spell
to write my poem about being a mongrel
I must love even the fox that impedes my path
n jettison my former ire n any gesture toward abstraction
n go to the dump finally w/ the disused bicycle tires and the broken antlers
    and the cracked stained glass of a ship that formerly I wdve harbored because
    I did not love myself
but the broken shelf
I want namore of it
the jangle-mongrel and the rose and the ndn cowboy that layall closeted
along w/ my availability to my own mind and the killings of our familyes queer
    and black and brown and ndn
slaughter at orlando symbol of our hermitude
massacre at aravaipa gashdla'á cho o'aa   big sycamore standing there
bear river sand creek tulsa rosewood
n when I finally sussed them out
n laid the tequila in its proper trash
n attempted to corral the pony of my mind
they say the ohlone were here as if
there were no more ohlone

erected a fake shellmound called it shellmound avenue

my friends dont like that

my friends dont like that excrement

it's not like youd give away the algorithm, my bf pointed out,

to the one yr tryin to put a spell on

marcabru uses the word 'mestissa' to describe the shepherdess his dickish
    narrator is poorly courting

which paden translates 'half-breed' and pound 'low-born' and snodgrass 'lassie'
    but I want to say mongrel, mestiza, mixedbreed

melissima most honeyed most songful

what catullus called his boyfriend's eyes

honey the color of my dead dog's eyes the stomach of the bee

I'm going to gather pollen from the cattails in a week or two

to pray to the plant tell it I'm only taking what I need

use a coathanger to hook the ones far from shore

filter it thru chiffon four times

what is love

but a constellation of significances

lyke-like magic

los cavecs nos aüra as the owl augurs

one gapes at a painting

the other waits for mahana

acknowledgments

Versions of these poems have appeared in *Big Bell*; *Cram*; *Denver Quarterly*; *Esque*; *580 Split*; *FUTURETAROT—The Black Moon*; *Jacket*; *Kite Full of Whiskey*; *Mrs. Maybe*; *Nepantla: A Journal Dedicated to Queer Poets of Color*; *No, Dear*; *Poets for Living Waters*; *Troubling the Line: Trans and Genderqueer Poetry and Poetics*; *Wheelhouse*; and on the blog *Herm of Warsaw*. Thank you to the editors.